Maisy is on her way to presc
Draw a line from Maisy to th

Start

POLICE

PIZZA

OPEN

FIRE STATION

Post Office

GAS

Biff's Garage

PRESCHOOL

Finish

Red

 Color the  red.

Circle the picture that is **red**.

Yellow

 Color the  **yellow**.

 Circle the picture that is **yellow**.

Orange

 Color the 🎃 **orange**.

✏️ Circle the picture that is **orange**.

Green

 Color the  **green**.

 Circle the picture that is **green**.

Blue

 Color the  **blue**.

 Circle the picture that is **blue**.

Purple

Color the 🍆 **purple**.

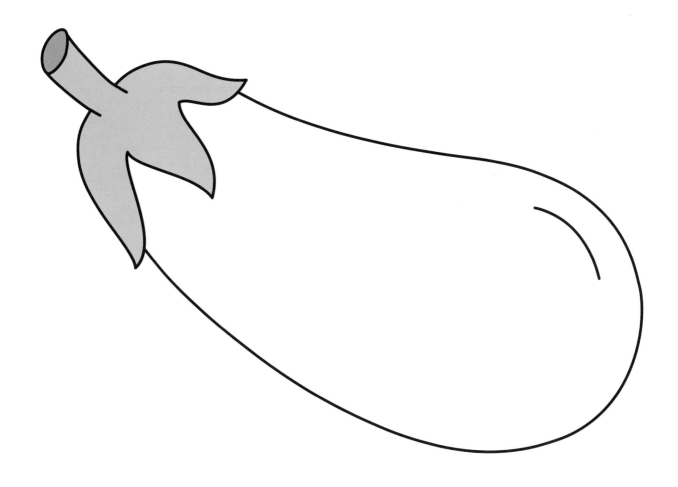

Circle the picture that is **purple**.

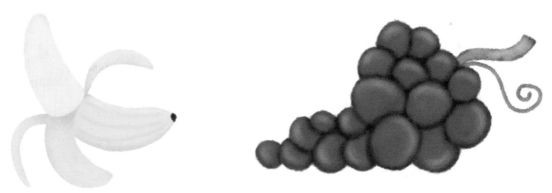

Brown

 Color the 🍪 **brown**.

 Circle the picture that is **brown**.

Black

 Color the  **black**.

 Circle the picture that is **black**.

9

 This is a **circle**.
Trace the circles.

 Color the circles.

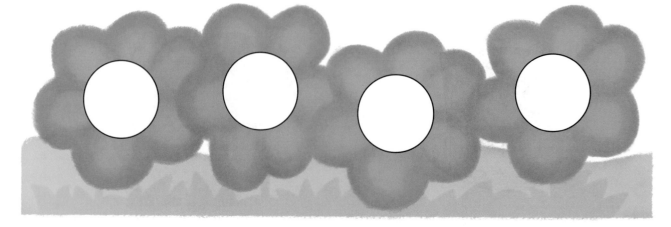

Trace the **circles**.
Color the circles orange.

 This is a **square**.
Trace the squares.

 Color the squares.

Trace the **squares**.
Color the squares blue.

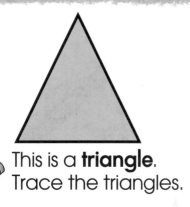

This is a **triangle**.
Trace the triangles.

Color the triangles.

Trace the **triangles**.
Color the triangles yellow.

Matching Shapes

 Draw lines to **match** the shapes.

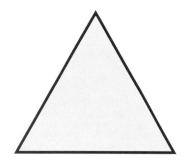

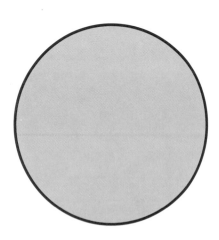

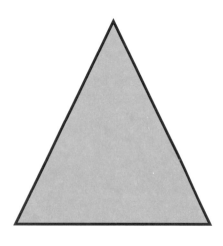

Draw lines to **match** the shapes.

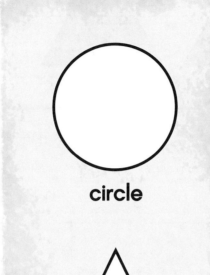

circle

triangle

square

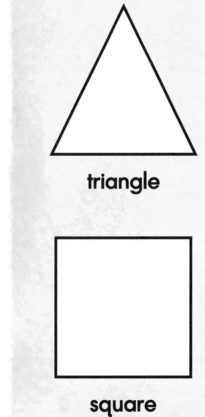

Same or Different

Same

✏️ Circle the shape in each row that is the **same size** and **shape** as the first one.

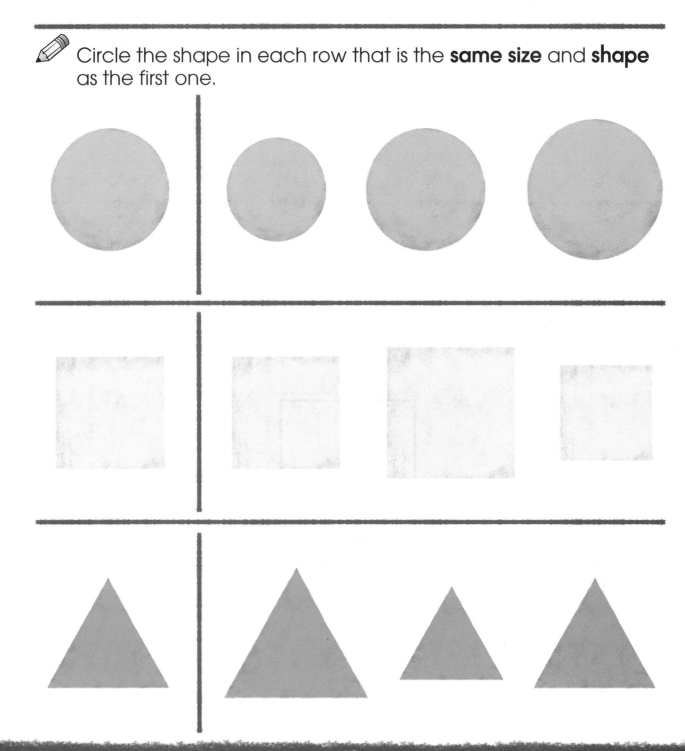

Draw lines to **match** the shapes.
Color the big shapes blue.
Color the small shapes **red**.

Same or Different

 Circle the shape that does **not belong**.

Circle the shape that comes **next**.

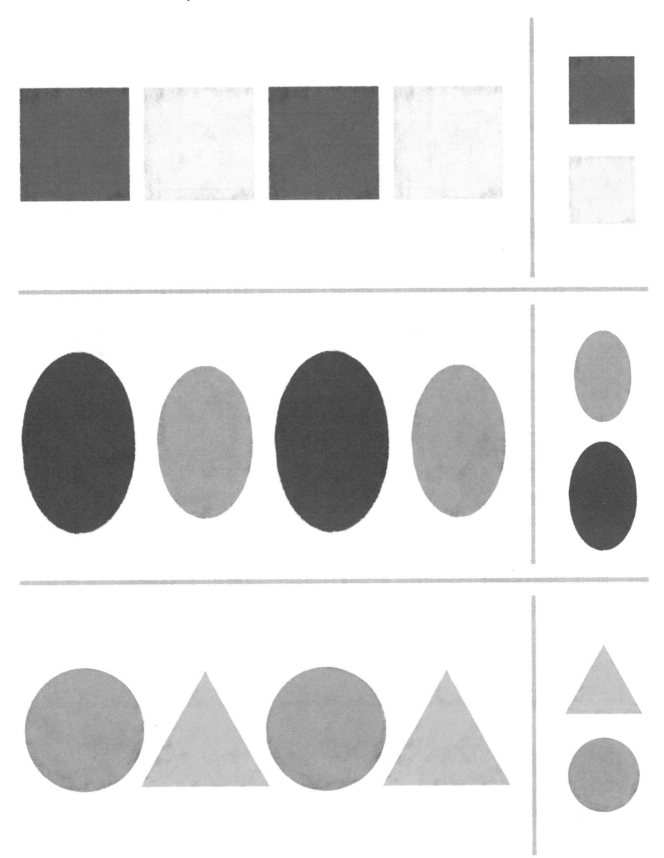

Opposites

little   **big**

 Draw lines to match the **opposites**.

slow

dry

wet

old

new

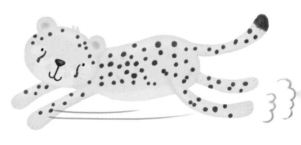

fast

Draw lines to match the **opposites**.

happy

big

empty

full

little

sad

Opposites

 Draw lines to match the **opposites**.

hot

quiet

day

cold

loud

night

Draw lines to match the **opposites**.

stop

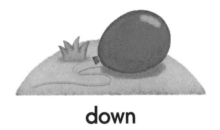

down

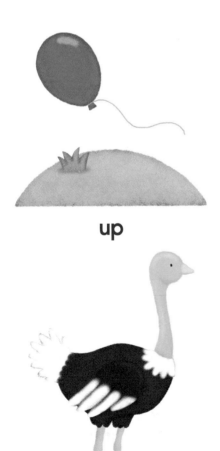

up

go

tall

short

Draw lines to match the **opposites**.

short

closed

open

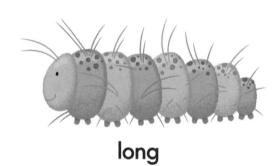

long

top

bottom

Draw lines to match the **opposites**.

on

back

front

out

in

What Goes Together?

 Look at the pictures in each row.
Circle the picture that **belongs** with the first one.

What Goes Together?

 Look at the pictures in each row.
Circle the picture that **belongs** with the first one.

 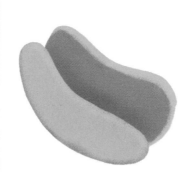 

What Goes Together?

 Look at the pictures in each row.
Circle the picture that **belongs** with the first one.

What Goes Together?

 Look at the pictures in each row.
Circle the picture that **belongs** with the first one.

Look at the pictures.
Circle the picture in each group that does **not belong**.

Look at the pictures.
Circle the picture in each group that does **not belong**.

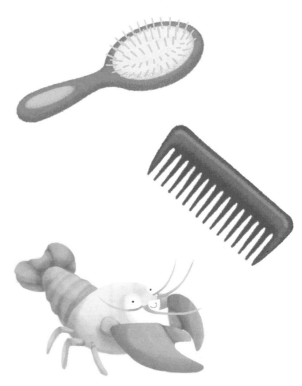

Same or Different

 Same  Different

 Look at the pictures in each row.
Circle the picture that is the **same** as the first one.

 **Same Color**  **Different Color**

 Look at the pictures in each row.
Circle the picture that is the **same color** as the first one.

Same or Different Shape

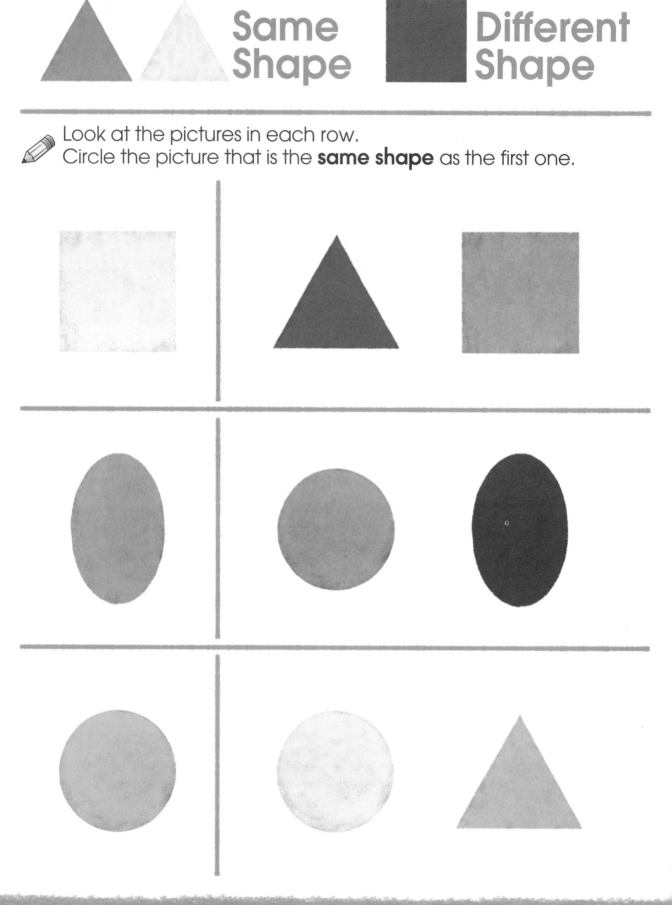

Same Shape

Different Shape

Look at the pictures in each row.
Circle the picture that is the **same shape** as the first one.

 **Same Size**

 **Different Size**

 Look at the pictures in each row.
Circle the picture that is the **same size** as the first one.

Same or Different Color

 **Same Color**    **Different Color**

 Look at the pictures in each row.
Circle the picture that is a **different color** from the first one.

 **Same Size**  **Different Size**

 Look at the pictures in each row.
Circle the picture that is a **different size** from the first one.

Same or Different

 Draw a line between the hats that are the **same**.
Circle the hat that does not have a match.

Draw a line between the socks that are the **same**.
Circle the sock that does not have a match.

Classification

Classification

 Draw lines from the pictures to where they **belong**.

Learning to Write

 Trace the lines from **top** to **bottom**.

Trace the lines from **left** to **right**.

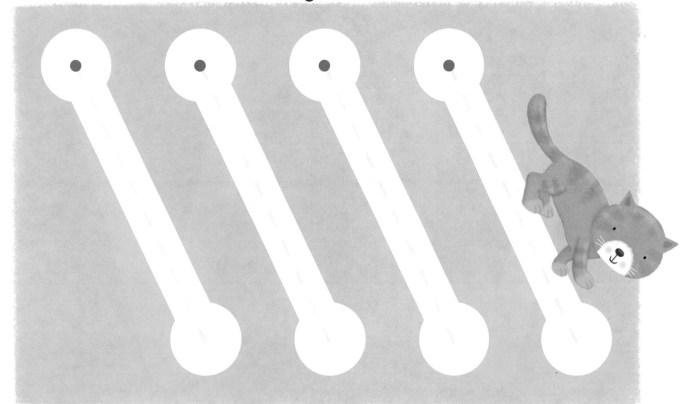

 Trace the lines from **right** to **left**.

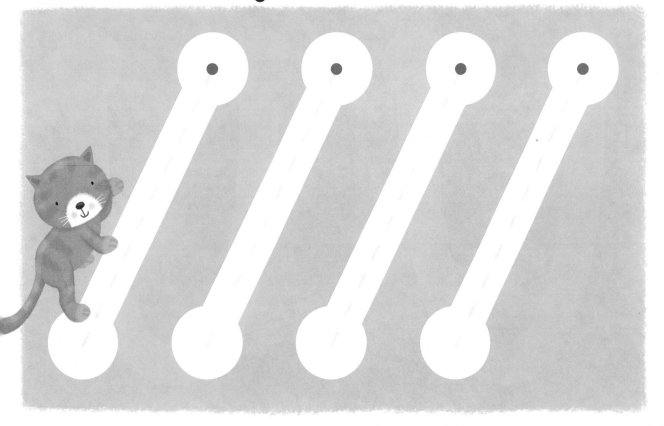

Learning to Write

✏️ Trace the lines from **left** to **right**.

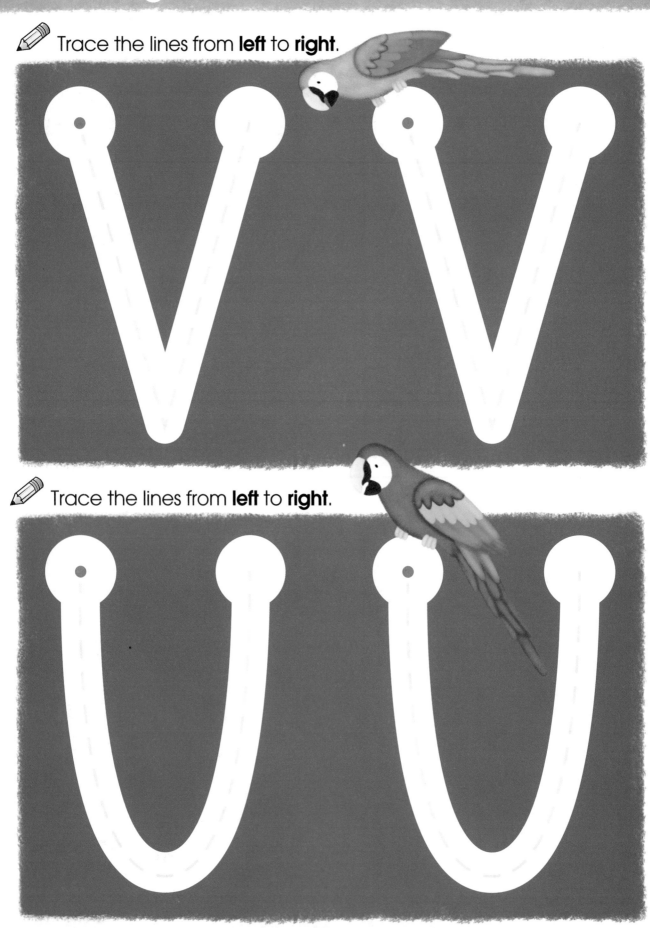

✏️ Trace the lines from **left** to **right**.

Trace the lines from **left** to **right**.

A

Ant

 Trace and write **A**.

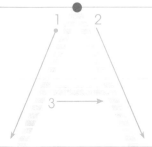

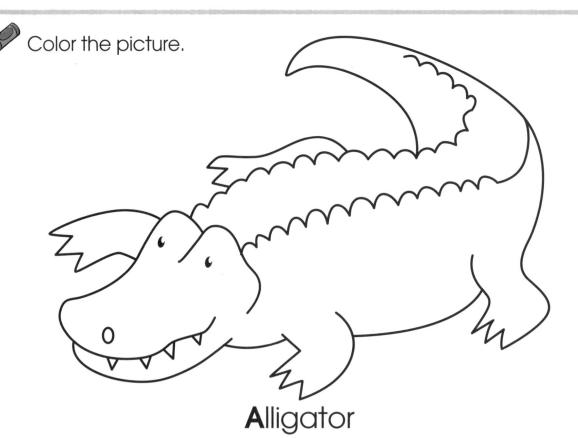 Color the picture.

Alligator

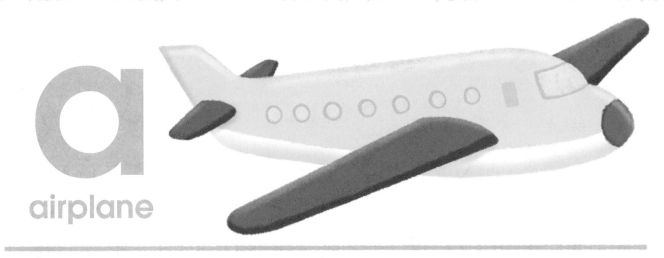

a
airplane

 Trace and write **a**.

 Circle the pictures that begin with **a**.

Say the name of each picture.
Color the pictures that begin with the letter **A**.

Help the alligator get to the pond.
Draw a line that shows the path.

Start

Finish

B
Bear

 Trace and write **B**.

Color the picture.

Ball

b

boat

 Trace and write **b**.

 Circle the pictures that begin with **b**.

Letters and Letter Sounds

 Say the name of each picture.
Color the pictures that begin with **B**.

SCHOOL BUS

Help Mrs. Bunny get home.
Draw a line that shows the path.

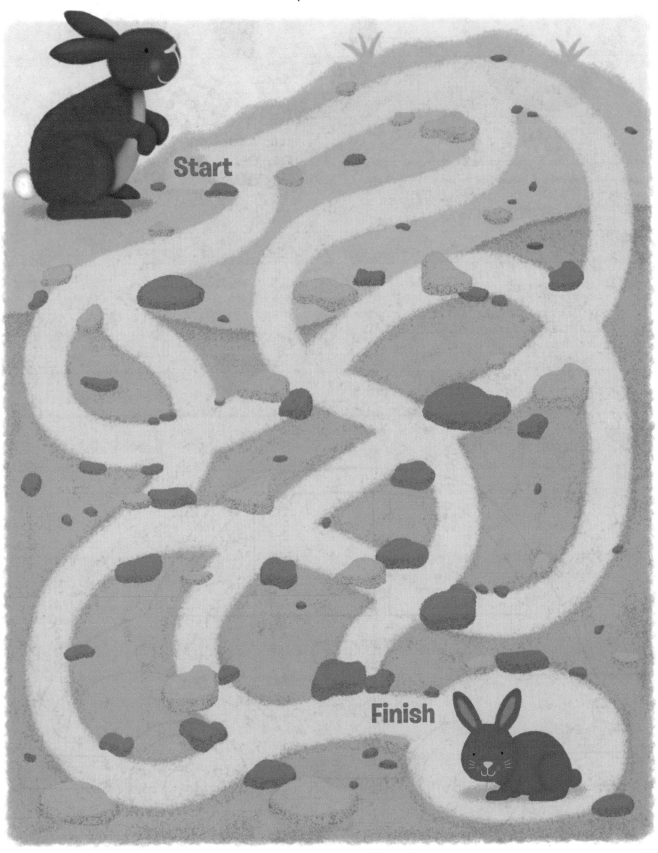

C

Cow

 Trace and write **C**.

Color the picture.

Car

C
camel

 Trace and write **c**.

Circle the pictures that begin with **c**.

Say the name of each picture.
Color the pictures that begin with **C**.

Help the cow get through the corn.
Draw a line that shows the path.

Start

Finish

D

Doll

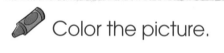 Trace and write **D**.

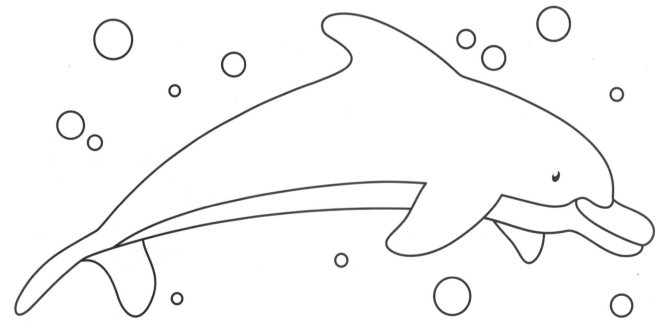 Color the picture.

Dolphin

d
dinosaur

 Trace and write **d**.

 Circle the pictures that begin with **d**.

Letters and Letter Sounds

 Say the name of each picture.
Color the pictures that begin with **D**.

Help the dog find his buried bone.
Draw a line that shows the path.

Start

Finish

Say the name of each picture.
Match the pictures to the **beginning** letter sounds.

A

B

C

D

Circle the pictures in each row that begin with the **same letter**.

E

Elf

✏️ Trace and write **E**.

1 2 →
3 →
4 →

🖍️ Color the picture.

Elephant

e

eggs

 Trace and write **e**.

 Circle the pictures that begin with **e**.

Letters and Letter Sounds

 Say the name of each picture.
Color the pictures that begin with **E**.

Help the elephant find its mother.
Color the footprints with the letter **E** or **e** on them to find the path.

Start

Finish

F

Fox

 Trace and write **F**.

 Color the picture.

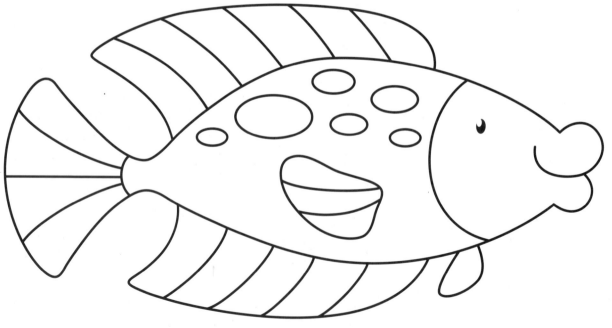

Fish

f

farm

 Trace and write **f**.

 Circle the pictures that begin with **f**.

Letters and Letter Sounds

 Say the name of each picture.
Color the pictures that begin with **F**.

Help the family of frogs find the pond.
Draw a line that shows the path.

G

Goose

 Trace and write **G**.

 Color the picture.

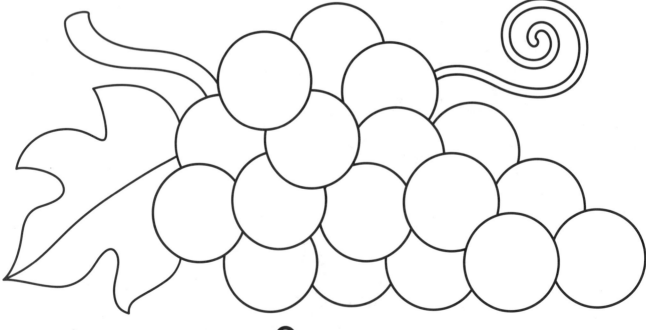

Grapes

g

grapes

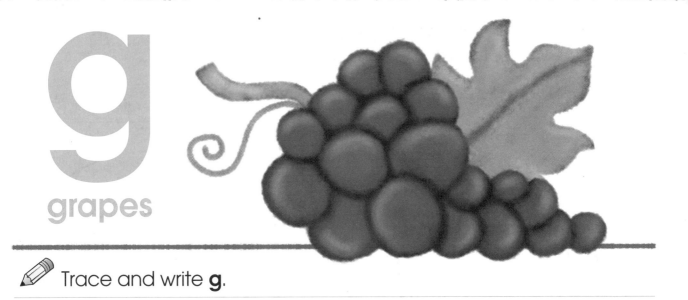

✏️ Trace and write **g**.

✏️ Circle the pictures that begin with **g**.

Say the name of each picture.
Color the pictures that begin with **G**.

Maze

Help the gorilla find his friend.
Draw a line that shows the path.

Start

Finish

H

Helicopter

✏️ Trace and write **H**.

1 2
3 →

🖍️ Color the picture.

Horse

h

hippo

✏️ Trace and write **h**.

✏️ Circle the pictures that begin with **h**.

Say the name of each picture.
Color the pictures that begin with **H**.

Help the horse find its way to the haystack.
Draw a line that shows the path.

Start

Finish

Say the name of each picture.
Match the pictures to the **beginning** letter sounds.

E

F

G

H

Circle the pictures in each row that begin with the **same letter**.

Igloo

 Trace and write I.

 Color the picture.

Iguana

i
insects

 Trace and write **i**.

 Circle the pictures that begin with **i**.

ink

Letters and Letter Sounds

 Color **I** and **i** on the .

Help the insects find their way home.
Draw a line that shows the path.

Start

Finish

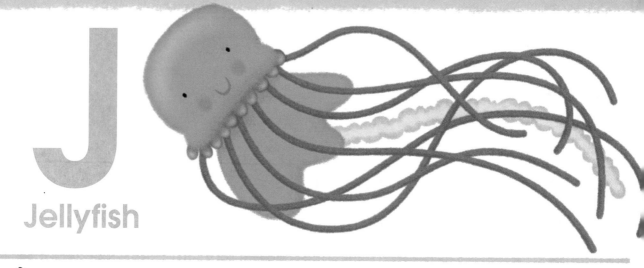

J

Jellyfish

 Trace and write **J**.

 Color the picture.

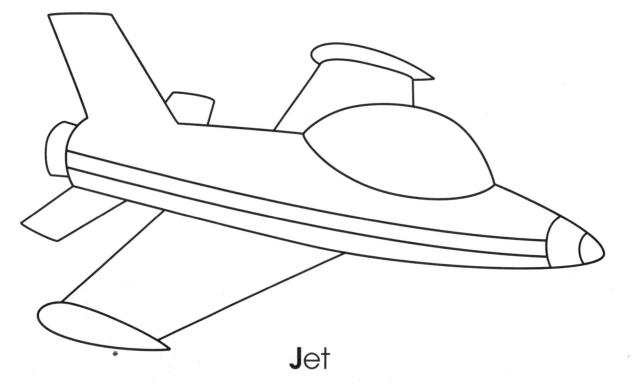

Jet

j
jaguar

 Trace and write **j**.

 Circle the pictures that begin with **j**.

Letters and Letter Sounds

Say the name of each picture.
Follow the pictures that begin with the letter **j** to solve the maze.

Help the jaguar find the way through the jungle.
Draw a line that shows the path.

Start

Finish

K

King

 Trace and write **K**.

 Color the picture.

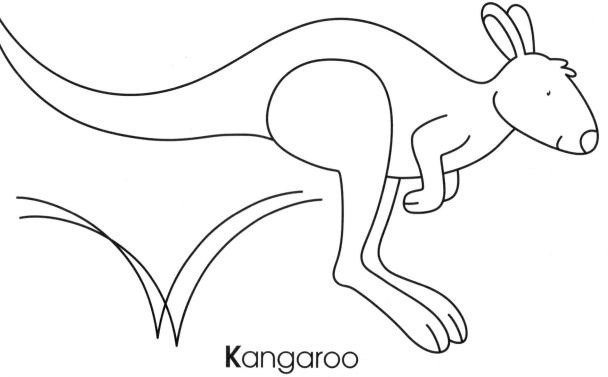

Kangaroo

k

koala

✏️ Trace and write **k**.

✏️ Circle the pictures that begin with **k**.

Say the name of each picture.
Color the pictures that begin with **K**.

Help the king find his way back to his kingdom.
Draw a line that shows the path.

Start

Finish

L
Lizards

✏️ Trace and write **L**.

1
2→

🖍️ Color the picture.

Lion

l

ladybug

 Trace and write l.

 Circle the pictures that begin with l.

Letters and Letter Sounds

 Say the name of each picture.
Color the pictures that begin with **L**.

Help the leopard find his lost friends.
Draw a line that shows the path.

✏️ Say the name of each picture.
Match the pictures to the **beginning** letter sounds.

I

J

K

L

Circle the pictures in each row that begin with the **same letter**.

M

Monkey

 Trace and write **M**.

1 2   4
      3

Color the picture.

Mouse

m
moose

✏️ Trace and write **m**.

✏️ Circle the pictures that begin with **m**.

Say the name of each picture.
Color the pictures that begin with **M**.

Help the monkey get to the merry-go-round.
Draw a line that shows the path.

Start

Finish

N
Net

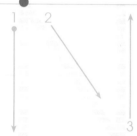 Trace and write **N**.

 Color the picture.

Nest

n
numbers

 Trace and write **n**.

 Circle the pictures that begin with **n**.

Say the name of each picture.
Color the pictures that begin with **N**.

Which bird will find her nest?
Trace each path to find the answer.

Letters and Letter Sounds

Ostrich

 Trace and write **O**.

Color the picture.

Owl

OX

 Trace and write **o**.

 Circle the pictures that begin with **o**.

Letters and Letter Sounds

Say the name of each picture.
Color the pictures that begin with **O**.

Help the owl and the otter get home.
Draw lines to show their paths.

Start

Start

Finish

Finish

P

Panda

 Trace and write **P**.

 Color the picture.

Puppy

p
penguins

 Trace and write **p**.

 Circle the pictures that begin with **p**.

Letters and Letter Sounds

Say the name of each picture.
Color the pictures that begin with **P**.

Help the penguin get to the pizza party.
Draw a line that shows the path.

Say the name of each picture.
Match the pictures to the **beginning** letter sounds.

M

N

O

P

Circle the pictures in each row that begin with the **same letter**.

Q

Quilt

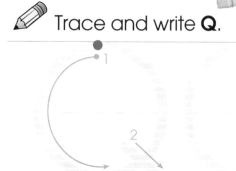

Trace and write **Q**.

1

2

Color the picture.

Queen

q
quail

 Trace and write **q**.

 Circle the pictures that begin with **q**.

Color the  with the letter **Q** or **q**.

Help the queen find her lost quarter.
Draw a line that shows the path.

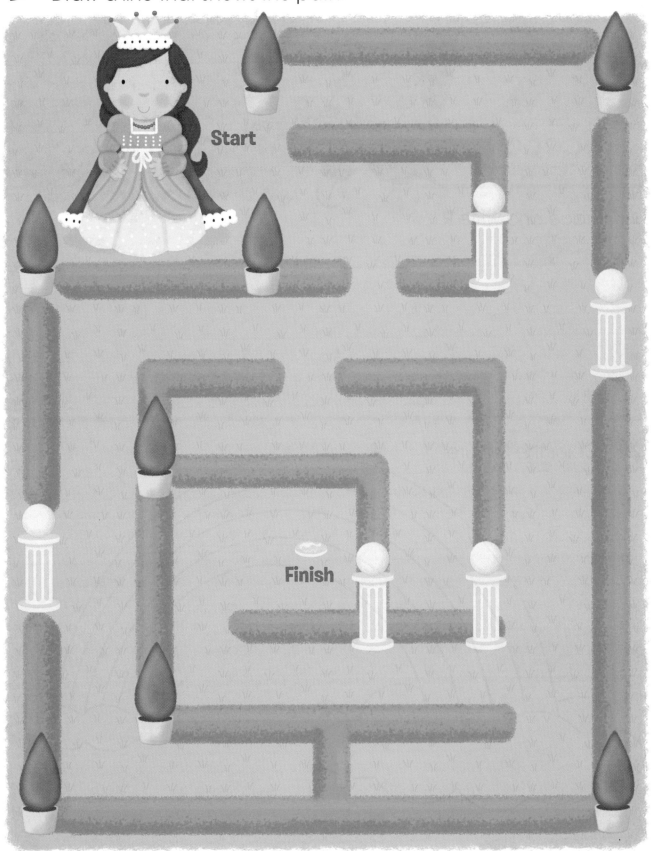

Start

Finish

Letters and Letter Sounds

R

Raccoon

✏️ Trace and write **R**.

R

✏️ Color the picture.

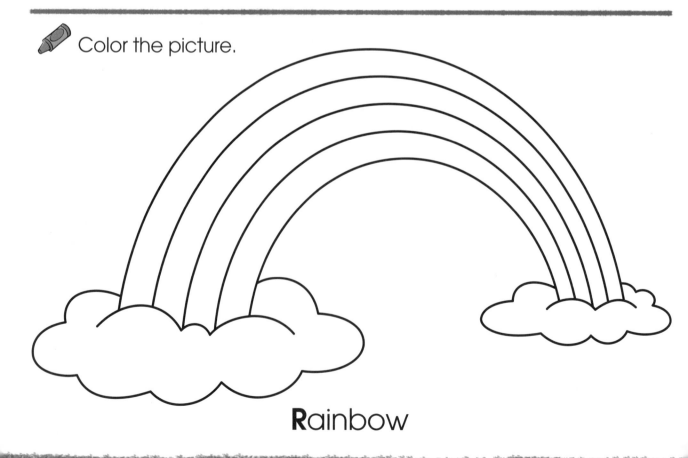

Rainbow

©School Zone Publishing Company 06361

r
rhino

 Trace and write **r**.

 Circle the pictures that begin with **r**.

Say the name of each picture.
Color the pictures that begin with **R**.

Help the rabbit get out of the rain.
Draw a line that shows the path.

Start

Finish

S
sun

 Trace and write **S**.

 Color the squirrel.

Squirrel

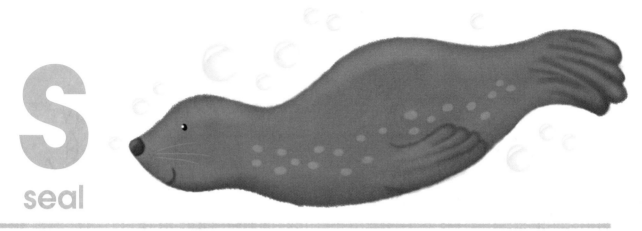

S

seal

 Trace and write **s**.

 Circle the pictures that begin with **s**.

Letters and Letter Sounds

Say the name of each picture.
Color the pictures that begin with **S**.

Help the sailor get to his sailboat.
Draw a line that shows the path.

Start

Finish

T

Turtle

🖉 Trace and write **T**.

🖍 Color the picture.

Tiger

train

 Trace and write **t**.

 Circle the pictures that begin with **t**.

Say the name of each picture.
Color the pictures that begin with **T**.

Help the train get to the town.
Draw a line that shows the path.

✏️ Say the name of each picture.
Match the pictures to the **beginning** letter sounds.

Circle the pictures in each row that begin with the **same letter**.

U
Underwear

✏️ Trace and write **U**.

🖍️ Color the picture.

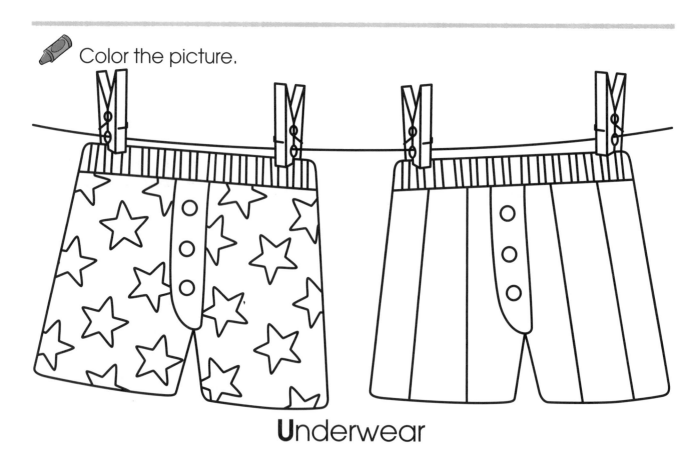

Underwear

u

umpire

 Trace and write **u**.

 Circle the pictures that begin with **u**.

Say the name of each picture.
Color the pictures that begin with **U**.

Help the girl get to her umbrella.
Draw a line that shows the path.

Start

Finish

V

Valentines

✏️ Trace and write **V**.

1   2

🖍️ Color the picture.

Van

V
volcano

 Trace and write **v**.

 Circle the pictures that begin with **v**.

Say the name of each picture.
Color the pictures that begin with **V**.

Help the rabbit get to each of the vegetables.
Draw a line that shows the path.

W

Walrus

✏️ Trace and write **W**.

✏️ Color the picture.

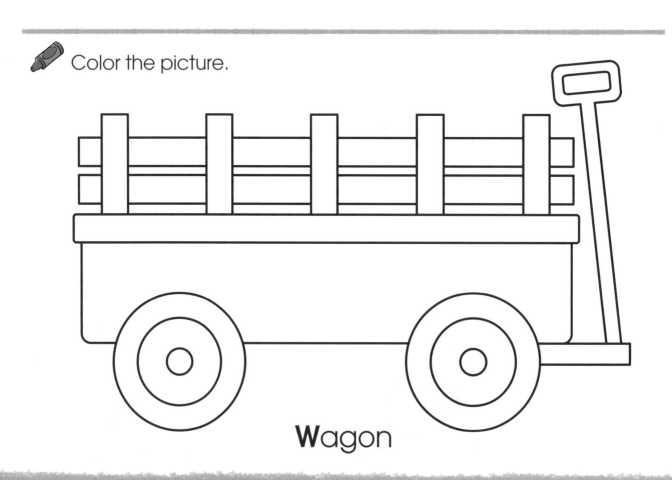

Wagon

watermelon

✏️ Trace and write **w**.

✏️ Circle the pictures that begin with **w**.

Say the name of each picture.
Color the pictures that begin with **W**.

Help the spider get through the web.
Draw a line that shows the path.

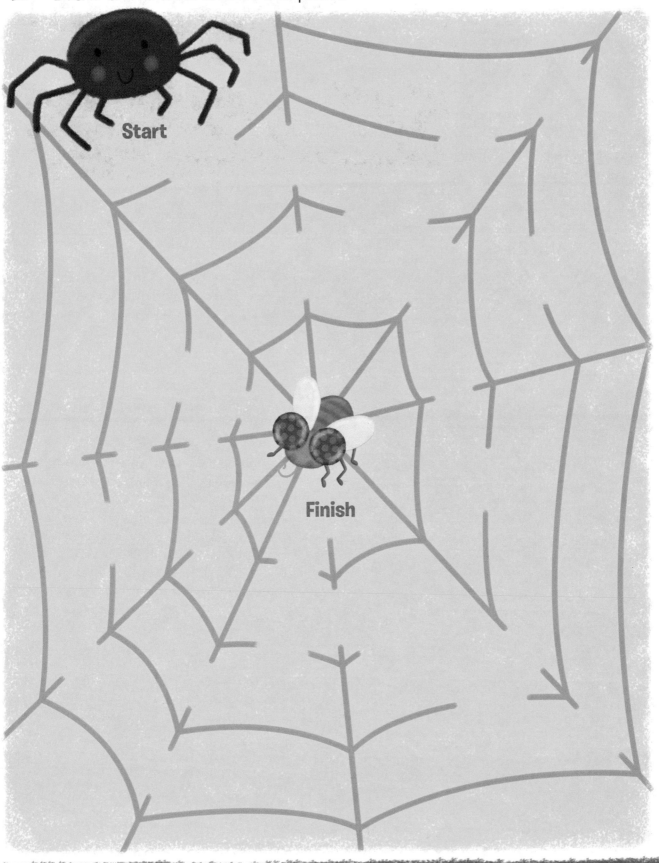

Start

Finish

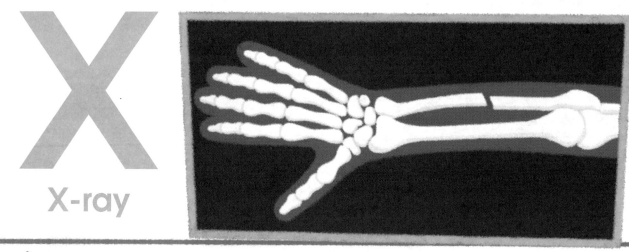

X

X-ray

 Trace and write **X**.

 Color the picture.

X marks the spot.

X
xylophone

 Trace and write **x**.

 Circle the pictures that begin with **x**.

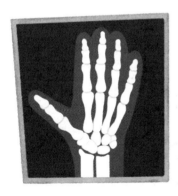

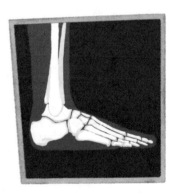

Letters and Letter Sounds

 Find and circle 8 **X**s in the picture.

Letters and Letter Sounds

 Help the sailor find the buried treasure.
Draw a line through the **X**s to show the way.

Start

X	W	Y	W	Z	Y
X	X	X	K	K	Y
Y	W	X	Y	W	Z
W	X	X	Z	Y	W
Y	X	Z	W	Y	W
W	X	X	X	X	Y

Finish

Y

Yarn

 Trace and write **Y**.

 Color the picture.

Yo-yo

yak

 Trace and write **y**.

 Circle the pictures that begin with **y**.

Say the name of each picture.
Color the pictures that begin with **Y**.

Help the yak get through the yard.
Draw a line through the **Y**s to show the way.

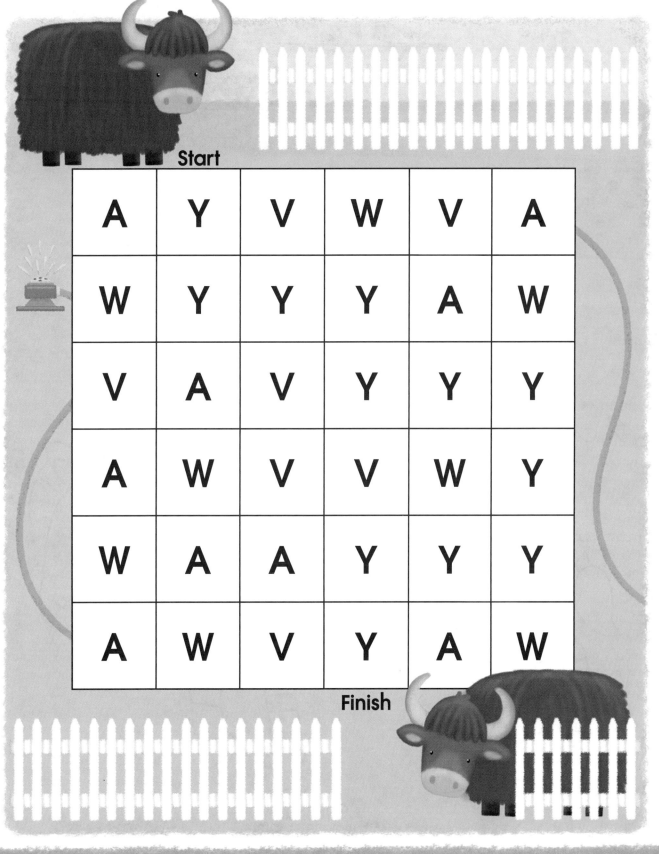

Start

A	Y	V	W	V	A
W	Y	Y	Y	A	W
V	A	V	Y	Y	Y
A	W	V	V	W	Y
W	A	A	Y	Y	Y
A	W	V	Y	A	W

Finish

Z

Zoo

 Trace and write **Z**.

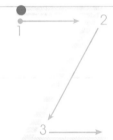

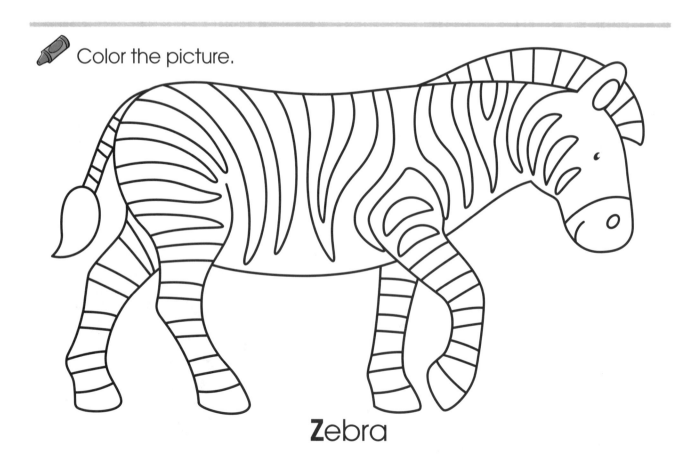 Color the picture.

Zebra

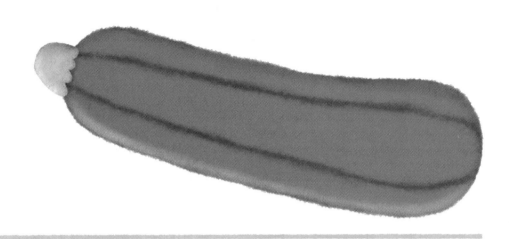

z

zucchini

 Trace and write **z**.

 Circle the pictures that begin with **z**.

Letters and Letter Sounds

 Say the name of each picture.
Color the **zoo animals**.

Help the zebra get to the zoo.
Draw a line that shows the way.

Start

ZOO

Finish

Review

 Find and circle the letters **U**, **V**, **W**, **X**, **Y**, and **Z**.

Follow the path of pictures from **u** to **z**.

Start

Finish

Review

 Connect the dots from **A** to **Z**.

 Color the picture.

Follow the letters from **A** to **Z** to get through the maze.
Draw a line that shows the path.

Say the name of each picture.
Circle the letter that **begins** its name.

c g d

k p h

b o r

q c m

Say the name of each picture.
Circle the letter that **begins** its name.

r p t

d b a

s n m

h k i

Say the name of each picture.
Circle the letter that **begins** its name.

b c a

s f e

g q d

b p y

Say the name of each picture.
Circle the letter that **begins** its name.

f   e   j

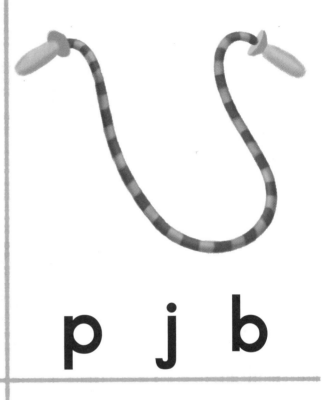

p   j   b

l   t   f

n   m   g

Beginning Sounds

 Circle the pictures in each row that begin with the **same sound**.

  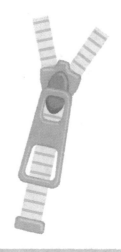

Circle the pictures in each row that begin with the **same sound**.

Beginning Sounds

 Circle the pictures in each row that begin with the **same sound**.

Circle the pictures in each row that begin with the **same sound**.

Beginning Sounds

 Circle the pictures in each row that begin with the **same sound**.

Circle the pictures in each row that begin with the **same sound**.

  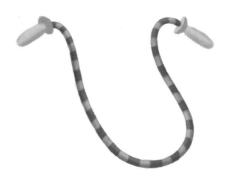

Beginning Sounds

 Circle the pictures in each row that begin with the **same sound**.

Circle the pictures in each row that begin with the **same sound**.

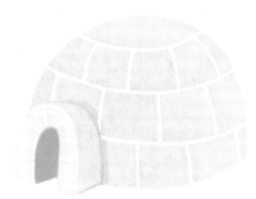

Beginning Sounds

 Circle the pictures in each row that begin with the **same sound**.

Draw a line from each letter to the picture that begins with the **same sound**.

Zz

Ff

Cc

Draw a line from each letter to the picture that begins with the **same sound**.

Rr

Uu

Ee

Draw a line from each letter to the picture that begins with the **same sound**.

Aa

Gg

Mm

Beginning Sounds

 Draw a line from each letter to the picture that begins with the **same sound**.

Oo

Pp

Ss

Draw a line from each letter to the picture that begins with the **same sound**.

Bb

Dd

Tt

Rhyming

 Say the name of each picture.
Check the two pictures that **rhyme** in each group.

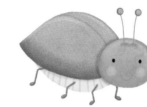

Say the name of each picture.
Check the two pictures that **rhyme** in each group.

Rhyming

Say the name of each picture.
Check the two pictures that **rhyme** in each group.

Say the name of each picture.
Check the two pictures that **rhyme** in each group.

Rhyming

 Say the name of each picture.
Check the two pictures that **rhyme** in each group.

Say the name of each picture.
Check the two pictures that **rhyme** in each group.

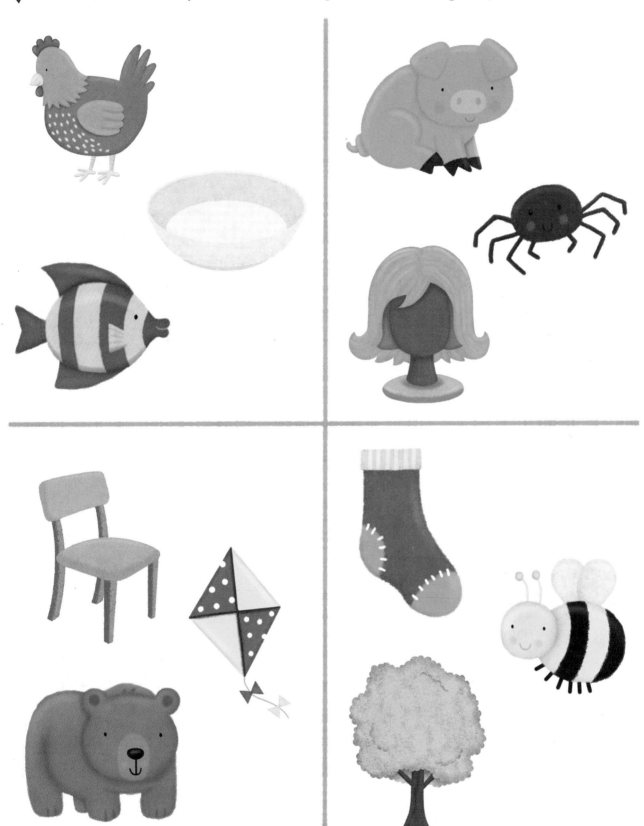

Rhyming

 Say the name of each picture.
Draw lines to match the words that **rhyme**.

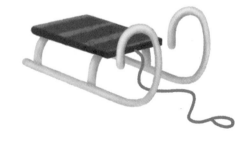

Say the name of each picture.
Draw lines to match the words that **rhyme**.

Numbers

Say the name of each number.
Trace the numbers **0-10**.

zero

 Trace and write **0**.

Color the frog with **0** spots.

1

one

Circle 1 picture in each group.

©School Zone Publishing Company 06361

Draw a line to match the **groups of** 1 to the number 1.

I

2

two

 Color the pictures to make **2** of each.

 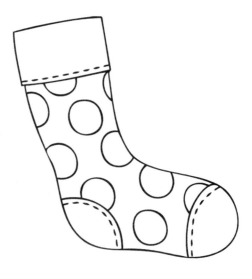

Draw a line to match the **groups of** 2 to the number **2**.

2

3

three

 Draw pictures so there are **3** things in each group.

Circle **3** pictures in each group.

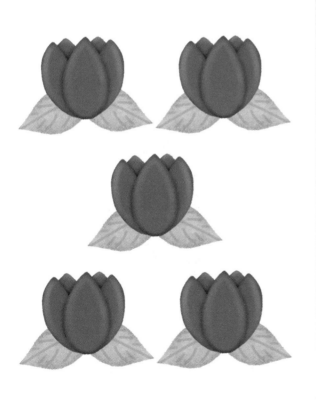

4
four

 Draw flowers to make **4** flowers in each row.

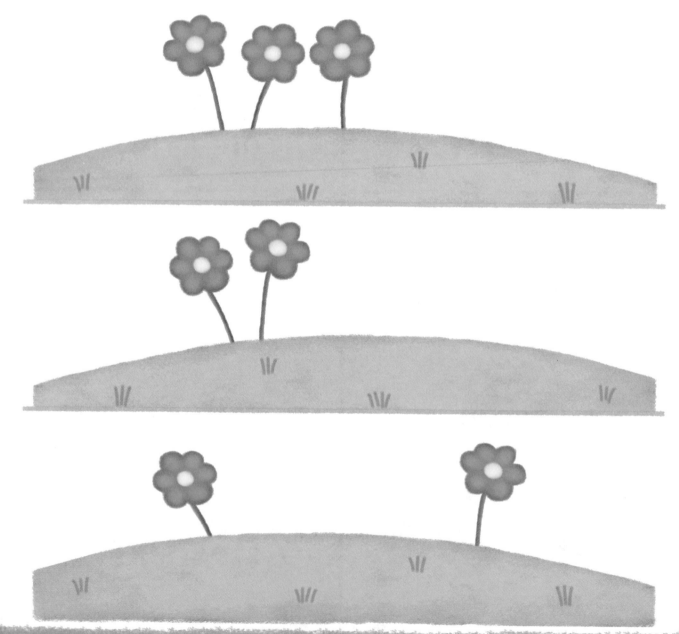

Draw a line to match the **groups of 4** to the number **4**.

5 five

Draw **5** 🍎 on the 🌳.

Draw a line to match the **groups of 5** to the number **5**.

Count the fish in each group.
Circle the number that tells **how many** there are.

3 4

4 5

2 4

2 3

Draw a line from the groups to the matching numbers.

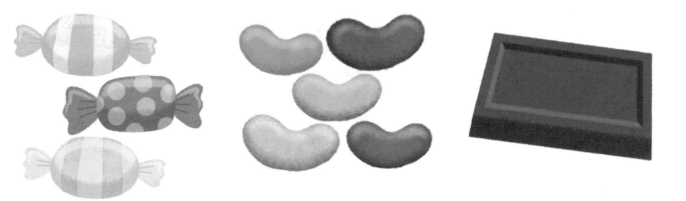

1 2 3 4 5

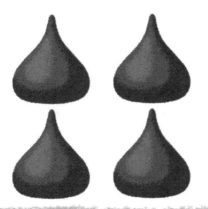

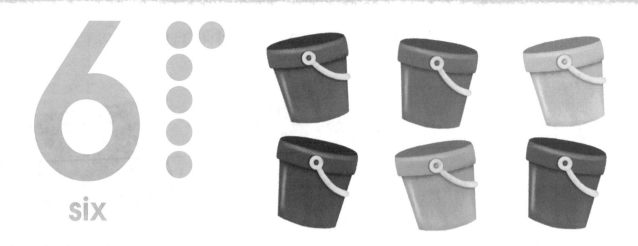

6 six

 Draw triangle sails on **6** boats.

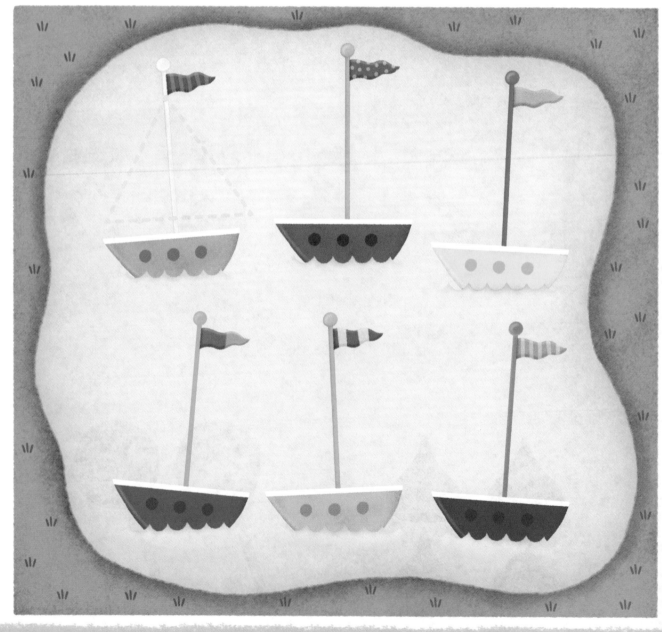

Draw a line to match the **groups of 6** to the number **6**.

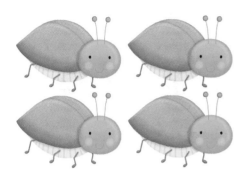

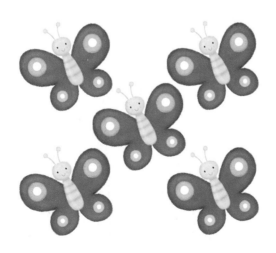

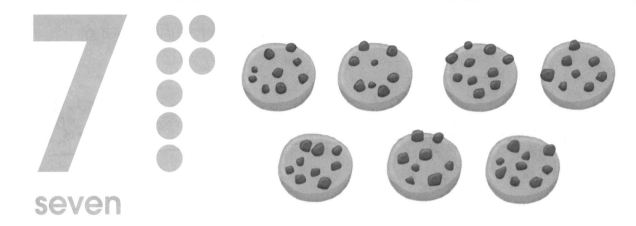

7

seven

 Color **7** of the kites.

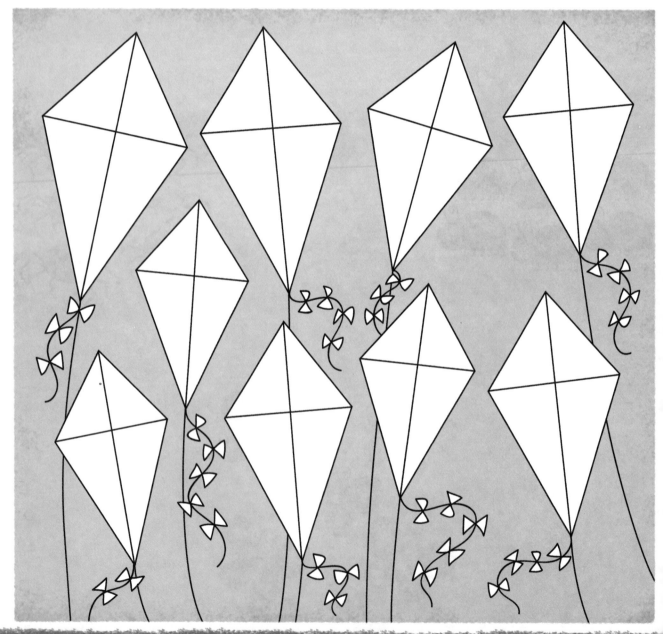

Circle **7** things on each shelf.

Numbers

8

eight

 Draw **8** legs on the spider.

Color **8** balloons.

9

nine

 Color **9** spots on the ladybug.

Draw a line to match the **groups of 9** to the number **9**.

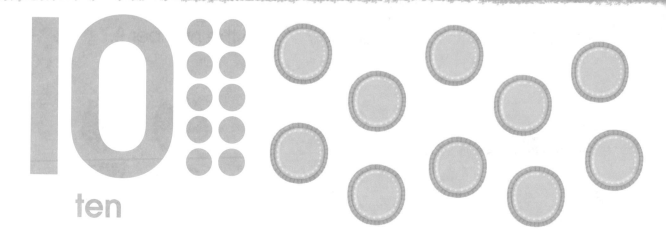

10

ten

 Draw **10** spots on the butterfly.
Color the butterfly.

Draw a line to match the **groups of 10** to the number **10**.

Count the bugs in each group.
Circle the number that tells **how many** there are.

6 7

8 9

7 8

9 10

Draw a line from each group to the matching number.

6 7 8 9 10

front   back

I penny = I¢

Count the pennies.
Write the number.

4¢   5¢

7¢   6¢

5¢   6¢

9¢   10¢

Count the pennies.
Write the number.

      = _____

       = _____

       = _____

Circle the picture in each group that costs **more**.

Circle the picture in each group that costs **less**.

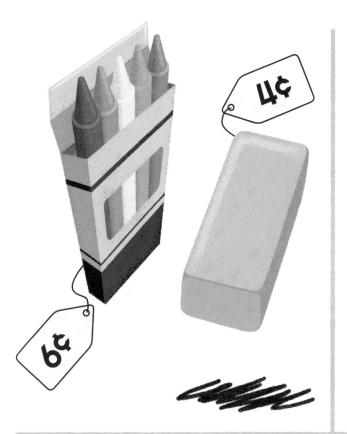

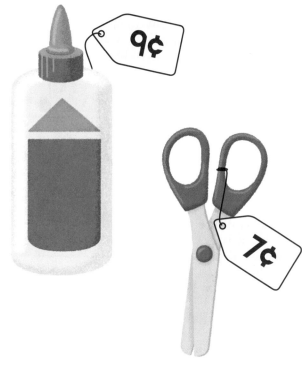

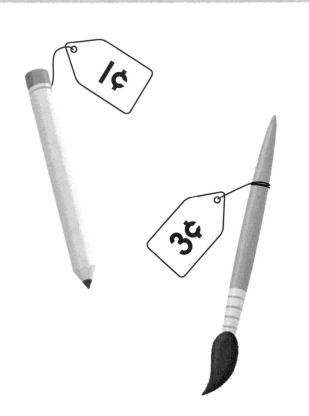

Numbers

Connect the dots from **0** to **10**.
Color the picture.

Help the rabbit find the carrots.
Follow the path of numbers from **1 to 10**.

Start

Finish

Numbers

✓ Find and check **6** in the picture.

Color the flower with **8** petals **red**.

Numbers

Circle the number that comes **before**.
The first one is done for you.

_ 3 4

1 (2)

_ 4 5

6 3

_ 5 6

3 4

_ 6 7

5 4

_ 7 8

6 8

_ 9 10

7 8

0 1 2 3 4 5 6 7 8 9 10

Circle the number that comes **after**.

1 2 ___	3 4 ___
3 4	6 5
2 3 ___	4 5 ___
5 4	3 6
5 6 ___	7 8 ___
7 8	9 10

Numbers

0 1 2 3 4 5 6 7 8 9 10

Circle the number that comes **between**.

1 __ 3

2 4

4 __ 6

3 5

5 __ 7

6 8

7 __ 9

8 10

8 __ 10

7 9

6 __ 8

5 7

228

©School Zone Publishing Company 06361

Connect the dots from **1** to **10**.
Color the picture.

Numbers

How many do you see on both pages?
Circle the number.

tiger	1	2	3
monkey	3	4	5
iguana	2	3	4

Add

Color 1 more 🎈.
Circle **how many** there are now.

1   2   3

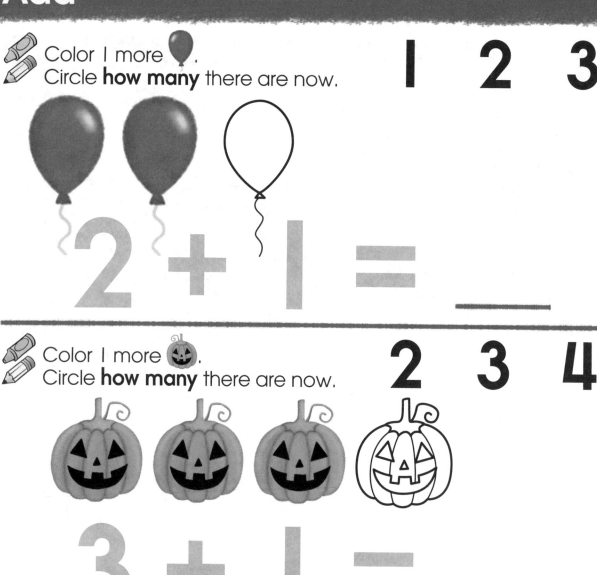

$$2 + 1 = \underline{\quad}$$

Color 1 more 🎃.
Circle **how many** there are now.

2   3   4

$$3 + 1 = \underline{\quad}$$

Color 1 more 🦋.
Circle **how many** there are now.

4   5   6

$$4 + 1 = \underline{\quad}$$

You ate 1 .
Circle how many **are left**.

1   2   3

$$2 - 1 = \underline{\quad}$$

 1  melted.
Circle how many **are left**.

1   2   3

$$3 - 1 = \underline{\quad}$$

 Three  are broken.
Circle how many **are left**.

1   2   3

$$4 - 3 = \underline{\quad}$$

Missing Parts

 Look at the pictures. Each butterfly is missing something. Draw and color what is missing.

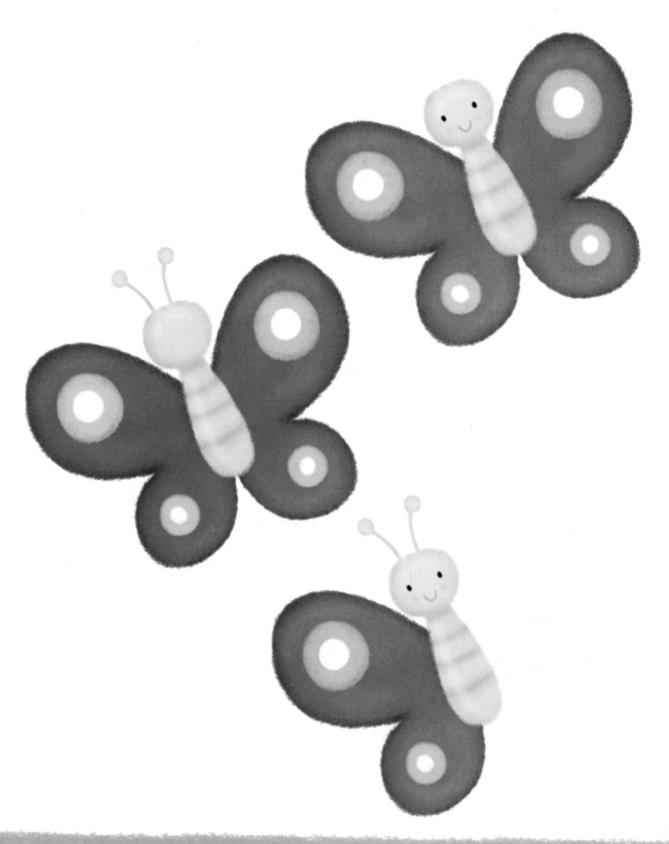

Look at the pictures. Each fish is missing something.
Draw and color the missing part.

Positional Words

 Circle the toy **next** to the .

 Circle the toy **above** the .

 Circle the toy **below** the .

 Circle the toy **next** to the .

Positional Words

Circle the animal **next** to the .

Circle the animal **above** the .

Circle the animal **below** the .

Circle the animal **next** to the .

Sequencing

 Write **1** by what happened **first**.
Write **2** by what happened **next**.
Write **3** by what happened **last**.

Write **1** by what happened **first**.
Write **2** by what happened **next**.
Write **3** by what happened **last**.

Matching Actions

Look at the pictures.
Draw a line between the **same actions**.

hop

walk

run

dig

Look at the pictures.
Draw a line between the **same actions**.

swim

jump

flying

swing

Why did this happen?
Circle the picture on the right that shows **why**.

Why did this happen?
Circle the picture on the right that shows **why**.

Patterns

 Circle the part of the **pattern** that is repeated.
The first one is done for you.

Color the fish to complete the **patterns**.

Patterns

 Color the pictures to complete the **patterns**.

Color the pictures to complete the **patterns**.

Emotions

happy

sad

 Circle the face you would make.

Circle the face you would make.

Senses

 Look at the pictures.
Circle the items you can **smell**.

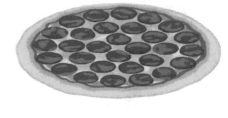

Look at the pictures.
Circle the items you can **taste**.

Senses

 Look at the pictures.
Circle the items you can **touch**.

Look at the pictures.
Circle the items you can **hear**.

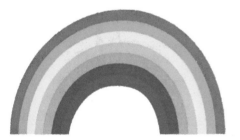

Community Helpers

People in our community have jobs that help us.
Look at the pictures.
Draw lines to match the workers to where they work.

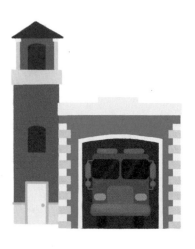

Look at the pictures.
Draw lines to match the workers to what they use for their job.

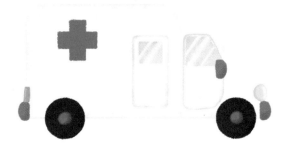

AWARD!

_____

Name

finished

Get Ready For Preschool

from

School Zone Publishing Company.

Get Ready For Preschool 06361